Praise for C

"Up there with the most inspiring, kick-arse books I have ever read."

Krystal Abbott

"Having trouble putting it down. Actually, it's not trouble at all as I'm enjoying every minute of it. Awesome read by someone who got their shit together and took the time to show me exactly how."

David Scott Kane

"Read it from cover to cover in my tent last night. Get out of my head Dan Norris! Seriously, thank you. Time to get back to creating something..."

Matt Rosinski

"*Create or Hate* is a modern-day Zen master's guide to creativity."

Joella Castillo

"Amazing read by one of the most effective, productive people I know!"

Glen Thomson

"Totally inspiring, It's the first book I've read start to finish in one day. Thank you for making something so easy to digest as well as thought provoking."

Kylah Morrison

"I love this new book from Dan Norris. For anyone that wants to create something in their life (i.e. everyone), this is a must read. It's short but powerful."

Michaela Clark

"When I sat down to write about success, I wrote—and re-wrote—and re-wrote—and gave up. I couldn't put the words in the right order. I gave up and read a book instead. The book was *Create Or Hate*. It's a short read and serendipitously included a section on success that says everything I wanted to say, only far more eloquently. I enjoyed it very much, and I think you will, too.

Matthew Kimberley

Join Other Creatives and Entrepreneurs in My Free Facebook Group

When I wrote my first book, *The 7 Day Startup*, I gathered a few of my favorite people in a Facebook group to help spread the news. It turned into an awesome place where we all helped each other with our creative and entrepreneurial projects.

Over 10,000 people have joined the group, and I'd love for you to join also.

Every day, we dissect different topics around creativity, online marketing, and entrepreneurship.

Type '7 Day Startup' into Facebook and request to join the group called "The 7 Day Startup (open)" and I'll add you in. See you in there!

CREATE OR HATE

CREATE OR HATE

SUCCESSFUL PEOPLE MAKE THINGS

DAN NORRIS

Published by Dan Norris
http://dannorris.me
The moral right of the author has been asserted.

First Printing, 2016

Cataloguing-in-Publication entry is available
from the National Library of Australia.

ISBN: 9780995404441 (paperback)
        9780995404458 (ebook)

Front cover design by Camille Manley
Internal design by Brett Geoghegan

Create something today.

TABLE OF CONTENTS

CONTENTS

CREATE OR HATE

CHAPTER 1

SUCCESSFUL PEOPLE MAKE THINGS

"There are people who make things happen,
there are people who watch things happen,
and there are people who wonder what happened."

—Jim Lovell

I had a dream last night. In my dream, I was a stick figure in a black-and-white story. Not a story in a book, but on a large canvas. The kind that could go on forever, as long as someone kept adding to it.

Luckily for my stick figure self, that was my job—to go around, painting sections on the canvas around me, keeping it going.

I was holding a bright flower and walking around the off-white surface. As I walked into a new area, the lines of objects magically appeared underneath me, ready to be colored in. I could touch my flower to any of these sections and, in an instant, a burst of orange or other vibrant color would magically fill the space.

It was wonderful and exciting. Anything was possible, and it was all up to me.

I walked around filling the spaces between the lines with color, gradually making a beautiful masterpiece.

After a while, a shadow appeared. It was a grey-colored version of me that followed me everywhere I went. He held a grey flower and every time I tapped my flower on the canvas, he tapped his flower on my flower, causing it to become less vibrant.

He wasn't aggressive and he didn't show emotion; it was just like he had a job to do.

From then on, whenever I tapped my flower onto the rolling canvas, the resulting color was less vibrant. Every time the shadow tapped my flower, the color would fade even more. I continued around the story, tapping the sections and watching the colors from my flower fade.

Eventually my flower turned completely grey and no longer painted color into the story. Since everything I painted was dull and colorless, I just stopped.

WHAT HAVE YOU NOT CREATED YET?

"Making art hurts. But it's better than the alternative."

—Seth Godin.

Most of us have always wanted to make something, but for any number of reasons haven't.

What is that something for you? Writing a book? Creat- ← ①
ing a blog? Learning photography? Building a house? Painting a canvas? Starting a podcast? Launching a business?

There must be something you want to make, or else you
wouldn't have picked up this book.

This book exists for only one reason. I believe that the
world will be a better place if you create what you want to
create. I believe you will be happier, more fulfilled, and maybe even more successful if you create something.

The problem is that there are forces working against you.
Barriers that are stopping you from breaking through to the
creative side of life. If this wasn't the case, you'd already be
creating.

This book exists to help you remove those barriers, or at
least temporarily lower them.

This book exists to help you create something TODAY.

WHAT I'VE LEARNED ABOUT SUCCESS

"Everything around you was created by people who were no smarter than you."

—Steve Jobs

There's a reason I wrote a book about how to create more, instead of a book about how to be successful.

Success is random and unpredictable.

Even successful people don't know how they became successful. Most of them say it's because of 'hard work'. They think they work harder than others who aren't as successful. In truth, they probably don't—you are probably working just as hard.

I left a good job at 26. I owned a house in the best suburb in the city, I was in love and about to be married. I was on a pathway to entrepreneurial riches. I was so confident, that when I left my job, I actually told my co-workers that I would be a millionaire by the age of 30.

By 33 I was broke, owned nothing, had no business, was soon to be divorced, was diagnosed with anxiety and depression, and had been prescribed three different meds for Attention Deficit Hyperactivity Disorder (ADHD).

Now I just call it 'being an entrepreneur,' but at the time, it was pretty scary. What was worse, I found myself applying for jobs at companies similar to where I used to work!

I'd risked it all and worked my arse off for seven years chasing the dream of entrepreneurship.

Everything I'd done had failed; I was a joke. My friends from my old job, who were younger and less qualified, had earned more than me every year since I had left. My entrepreneurial friends were no smarter or more experienced than me, but they were firing solutions at me like I was a kid.

They were right. I was trying everything and working on three things at once, desperately seeking that elusive key to success.

In the three years that followed, I kept to the same strategy, even though everyone told me it was wrong. I worked on a bunch of things at once, launched different businesses, created a lot of content, and tried to make entrepreneurship work.

By 36, I was a millionaire off the back of one of my entrepreneurial projects, a WordPress support business called WP Curve. I launched it in seven days because that was all the time I had left before I ran out of money. I'd been writing blog posts the whole time, thinking that one day my content would build enough trust to get the attention I needed to make it as an entrepreneur.

It turns out I was right.

Within two years, WP Curve was turning over one million USD a year and had become a leading example of how to productize service businesses around the world. My co-founder, Alex, suggested I write a book about it, so I got busy and wrote it.

It's called *The 7 Day Startup*. It was a #1 Amazon best-seller, selling 30,000+ copies, and was translated into six languages. More importantly, it started a movement that encouraged other entrepreneurs to launch their projects instead of procrastinating. It inspired many to build what are now 6-and-7 figure businesses. Because people wanted to learn more, I created an online community. Within months, I had hundreds of people paying me a membership subscription.

I'd built WP Curve without spending a cent on advertising, using content marketing alone. Because of the business's success, I was now considered an authority on content marketing. Brett, who worked in the office next to me, said I should write a book about that, so I did. It's called *Content Machine*, has sold over 15,000 copies, and has been translated into three languages.

Between the books and the online community, I had built another six-figure business on the side.

Then, I started getting interested in craft beer and, because of my business smarts, my mates wanted my involvement in an idea they had to make an Eggnog Stout. We made it and turned that into a business as well, becoming Australia's first brewery to launch via crowdfunding. We also worked with the *Call of Duty*® video game brand to make the world's first *Call of Duty*® beer, and opened a brewery on the Gold Coast in Australia.

That was my third six-figure business since my rock-bottom moment a few years earlier.

I was a bestselling author now, so it made sense for me to write a book on our experiences setting up the brewery. It's called *Operation Brewery* and it is rapidly becoming another Amazon best seller. It's become a bible for entrepreneurs looking to start their own craft beer breweries.

During this window of success, I started speaking at conferences, despite having severe social anxiety. People wanted to hear my story, which resulted in me becoming a well-known speaker at international entrepreneurship events. I travelled internationally, from Bangkok to Sydney to the Philippines, delivering speeches for up to 600 people.

I started thinking about the keys to success.

Hard work? I'd worked my arse off up until the age of 33, and now was just cruising. It couldn't be that.

Persistence? I had worked on something for seven years

that only started becoming successful once I gave up on it. It couldn't be persistence.

Domain expertise? I started a brewery for fuck's sake. I knew nothing about beer, besides the fact that I enjoyed drinking it—not exactly a unique skill amongst Australians!

There are a lot of factors that go into success.

Timing is a huge factor that is rarely acknowledged and can often be the difference between complete failure and monumental success. What a person starts with, who their friends are, and what they have access to are all factors that determine success.

When I look at my success and the successes of others, it's pretty clear that the majority of the factors are completely random.

I couldn't write a book about being successful, because there is no universal truth to being successful. There is no blueprint to success.

The only thing I do know about successful people is that they create things.

Steve Jobs made computers. Henry Ford made cars. Walt Disney made cartoons. Richard Branson made records. Elon Musk makes rockets. Oprah makes TV shows. J.K. Rowling makes books. Bill Gates makes software. The list goes on, and on, and on.

I can't tell you how to be successful. But I can tell you that if you don't make anything, you won't be successful.

Successful people make things.

PRODUCTIVITY = CREATIVITY

"If you are alive, you are a creative person."

—Liz Gilbert

My girlfriend, Emma, was at a conference recently and the person on stage said, "Who are the creative people here! Throw your hands up!" Of course, people were reluctant to put their hands up because calling yourself creative is a big deal! It's like the difference between calling yourself self-employed and calling yourself an entrepreneur.

Call yourself an entrepreneur, and you better change the world in a big way.

I was in business for 10 years before I admitted that I was an entrepreneur. It wasn't until I was actually getting good results and approval from my peers that I accepted it. But of course, I was an entrepreneur the whole time.

Creativity is similar. A lot comes along with the label 'creative person'. People are reluctant to own up to it because there's this misconception that you are either gifted in some magical creative way, or you aren't.

Creativity is greatly misunderstood.

According to Robert Sutton, author and Professor of

Management Science and Engineering at Stanford School of Engineering, "Creativity isn't about wild talent as much as it's about productivity. To find a few ideas that work, you need to try a lot that don't. It's a pure numbers game." Being creative isn't magic. It's just a person deciding to create.

Liz Gilbert, author of *Eat, Pray, Love* and my favorite book, *Big Magic*, says, "If you are alive, you are a creative person." I tend to agree. Everyone is creative, but not everyone knows it, and of course, not everyone uses their creativity.

When I was in high school, I took a drama class because, other than religion, it seemed like the least amount of work. Turns out I did have to work. I had one job. My class was to put on a play called "Wolf Boy," and my job was marketing.

I did nothing for an entire semester, until the day before the performance, when I printed off a photo of a wolf from Microsoft Encarta (an old school, pre-internet digital multimedia encyclopaedia), put the play details on it, and gave it to my friend to hand out. I didn't even bother turning up!

That's the least creative person the world has ever seen right there. I didn't know I was creative then. I couldn't paint, I couldn't write well, I couldn't play instruments well, I couldn't hold a pen straight, so I sucked at graphics, I couldn't sing, I couldn't dance, I obviously wasn't the best drama student, and I couldn't even get into the woodworking class.

But all of that didn't mean I wasn't creative. Because, as it turns out, in certain areas I *can* create things that people find interesting and useful. I just didn't know it yet. With a musician for a mother and an accountant for a father, I've found a sweet spot as a creative entrepreneur. Who would have thought?

In addition to the misguided view that creativity equates to talent, the other misconception about creativity is its correlation with massive success. People often place pressure on themselves to produce instant hits.

Want to call yourself creative? Then you'd better paint something epic, or have a number one single, or design an award-winning building, or write a bestselling book.

When we finally make something, we tend to turn to the people around us to decide whether it's good or not. The idea that the few people who surround you at this tiny moment in human history get to decide whether or not you are creative is a little bit crazy.

History is littered with people whose work was not considered great by the people around them.

Moby Dick received mostly negative reviews; its author Herman Melville was identified as Henry Melville in his obituary. JK Rowling received a ton of rejections for her first book, a little story called *Harry Potter and the Philosopher's Stone*. Vincent van Gogh famously sold just one or two pieces of art in his lifetime, dying penniless and alone. Bach, that guy who wrote some of the most famous works of classical music in the world, made most of his money as a church and event organist.

Humans have lived for 200,000 years. Approximately 107,602,707,791 (at the time of writing this) people have lived before you, and hopefully a lot more will live after. Don't write yourself off just because your creations aren't immediately successful, or aren't considered great by the people who surround you.

The bottom line is this: If you are creating things, then you are creative. If you aren't creating things, something is stopping you.

I call that something 'Hate'.

CHAPTER 2

MEET HATE

CREATOR + HATER

*"Our doubts are traitors, and make us lose the good
we oft might win, by fearing to attempt."*

—William Shakespeare

We know that we are all creative — that in each one of us there is a creator.

Someone who wants to use their head and their hands to make the story better. It's been that way since the dawn of human civilization. It's been that way for you since you were a kid, gleefully discovering the world and learning by trial and error that you can impact it in a magical way.

But there is also a force called Hate, which will work against your creativity.

Hate stops you from making things. Hate wasn't there at the start. It's been given power over the years and is now equipped with an arsenal of weapons designed to stop your creative self from making things.

Hate doesn't get joy from stopping your creative efforts, it just does its job.

Remember the shadow self stick figure from my dream, that was following my beautiful flower art trying to dull and eventually kill all the color from my creation? Creative, meet Hate.

Yet Hate can be controlled, managed, and overpowered if you know how.

THE BIRTHPLACE OF HATE

"It's easy to attack and destroy an act of creation. It's a lot more difficult to perform one."

—Chuck Palahniuk

Hate wins when you choose not to make things.

It doesn't happen all of a sudden; it happens gradually, starting out with simple, innocent negativity, which slowly escalates.

Ricky Gervais says, "It's better to create something that others criticize than to create nothing & criticize others." That's great, but the problem is it's much easier to criticize others than it is to create something yourself.

When you decide to jump on Facebook and whinge about something someone else made, you are immediately joined by other people who feel the same way. Why? Because it's easy and it makes people feel good about themselves. Jealousy is a powerful driver.

People don't want to admit that someone else made something, while they made nothing.

A lot of people aren't inspired by other people's success. Instead, they are overwhelmed and threatened by it. Jealousy and negativity kick in, and Hate rears its ugly head. Once you criticize something that someone else makes, you are under infinitely more pressure to make something great yourself. After all, you can't whinge about someone else's work and then produce something that's not significantly better. Right?

Haters don't create anything, and instead get caught up in a never-ending cycle of Hate feeding Hate and criticism triumphing over creation.

TWO WOLVES

"There are two wolves and they are always fighting.
One is darkness and despair, the other light and hope.
Which one wins? The one you feed."

—Cherokee Legend

Just as you can easily be dragged into the depths of Hate, you can also transition into a more creative place. Most of us are a reasonably even mix of both. Our thoughts, decisions, friends and environment dictate how much time we spend with each impulse.

If you hang around a bunch of negative people who only whinge about everything, your Hate will grow, and you will probably never create. The same goes if you decide to friend people on Facebook who are always pointing out negative things, or if you work in an environment full of pessimistic people.

What if you recognized every time someone was being negative, and chose not to entertain it at all? What if you only spent time with people who praise you for making things? What if you worked for yourself and didn't have any-one constantly telling you your work wasn't good enough?

If you don't allow Hate to feed and breed, you can turn

your focus to making things. Your creator can grow, despite the negativity.

There's a creator and a hater in each of us. You just need to decide which one you feed and which one you starve.

Any time you engage in negativity, you feed Hate and starve Create. Every time you make something and ignore negativity, you become a better creator and you starve Hate.

UP THE STAKES, BRING THE HATE

"Every man is guilty of all the good he did not do."

—Voltaire

The hater and creator are two competing forces that exist within you at all times.

Usually when the stakes are low, Hate is dormant. When the high-impact challenges present themselves and up the ante, Hate comes to life.

Posting a run-of-the-mill update to Facebook? Hate doesn't care. The stakes are low, and there's nothing to be fearful about, so Hate will give you that one.

About to hit publish on a blog post? The stakes are a bit higher. People might see it! What if it sucks? Hate is taking notice.

About to launch a book? Hate wants in. You aren't going on that journey alone.

About to speak in front of 1,000 people? If Hate lets you do this, you might feel so good after, that its very existence is in danger — at least for a bit. Hate is not going to let that happen. Hate is jumping in here, and working its hardest to stop you from ever speaking again.

The higher the stakes, the higher the reward, the more Hate wants control.

When you notice Hate, you should acknowledge it. We'll talk more about this later.

Feed your creative side and starve Hate so that when Hate does stand up, you are ready. This is the time when what you are doing might actually mean something.

THE WORST KIND OF HATE

"The worst enemy to creativity is self-doubt."

   —Sylvia Plath

When I first had the idea to write a book on creating, I asked my 7 Day Startup Facebook Group this question:

> "What do you wish you had created in your life up until this point? Be honest with your answer and tell me why you don't think you've done it yet."

I expected to get an OK response, because everyone tends to have at least one project that has gone unfinished. What I got was an outpouring of honest reflections about the real things that hold people back from action.

We know creating things is fun, personally rewarding, and sometimes very profitable. We know most of what we do with our time isn't any of those things. We know with absolute certainty that sitting around criticizing others who create is none of those things.

So logically, you would need a very good reason to not fulfill your creative urges, right?

Well, it turns out that people can be very good at making up reasons. Not all reasons are invalid, but we have to beware of Hate breeding excuses. Some of the things people talked about in that Facebook group post included:

> "It seems overwhelming to write enough to make up an actual book, and it's an expensive exercise, especially when you have to get editors and designers involved."

So Mary didn't write the book.

> "I feel like I've been waiting to do well enough in business, so I've avoided dividing my attention too much."

So James didn't launch a training course.

> "There's too much effort needed to start, and knowing I will definitely suck at the first try doesn't help. The learning curve will always be my stumbling block. When there's no purpose to get it going, it will never get started."

So Marilyn didn't learn photography and didn't make clay pots.

These real examples felt like legitimate reasons to not make stuff for the people who shared them. Reading between the lines, they were talked out of their creative aspirations by the worst kind of Hate. The kind that goes completely unchecked because it's not directed outward towards someone else. It's inward-directed, self-hatred.

You'd never talk that way about someone else, would you?

"Mary, you probably couldn't write enough quality prose to make a whole book. After all, you do suck. And since you're so weak and spineless, you're broke and couldn't afford to create a book. You'd need editors and designers too. As if!"

"James, please don't be one of those guys that teaches people something before they know it themselves. At least wait until you are successful before you attempt to to create something. Hypocrite!"

"Marilyn, listen. You don't have what it takes to start and you will most certainly suck. You are too dumb to learn and there's no point in doing it anyway. You will never get started."

Harsh words, right? Well, countless smart, educated, friendly, and ambitious people routinely allow the voice in their head to talk to them in this way. They let the Hate creep in, and give it 24/7 access to the command center that dictates their behaviour. Hate talks to them like they'd never talk to another person.

Yet you talk to yourself more than anyone else in your life. If you let the Hate say, "you can't, you shouldn't, you're too late, you're too dumb, you suck, and it won't work," then inevitably Hate will be right. You won't create, and you will be too late, and you will be too dumb, and you will suck and it won't work. Don't hand over the keys of control to the self-fulfilling prophecy of Hate.

Every self-help book ever written says that — believe it or not — what you tell yourself is what you become.

It is entirely counter-productive to give this kind of negativity free reign over your mind, but that's what many of us do.

Since Hate has 24/7 access to your brain, and — with this book — I only have a few hours at best, I will take the opportunity to provide the counter view to every fucking thing Hate says!

CHAPTER 3

FIGHT HATE

The first step in conquering Hate is to accept its presence and recognize it every time it rears its hideous head.

Hate is hard to spot, because it doesn't necessarily make you an angry, hateful person. It's action is more insidious, as it attacks your desire to make things, which is what you need to do to survive.

So how do you spot Hate?

Listen for that little voice in your head, telling you — in quite reasonable and measured tones — why you can't do something. The excuses that Hate comes up with often seem perfectly legitimate, which is why its influence can be hard to spot. Excuses are Hate's speciality.

Where there are excuses for failing to create, there's Hate.

DISARMING HATE

"If things are not failing you are not innovating enough."

—Elon Musk

Excuses are essentially lies.

Hate's strongest weapon is to convince you of things that aren't true, in order to stop you from making things.

Hate presents you with seemingly logical reasons for why you shouldn't do something. Most of the time the reasons are silly, but the mind has a funny way of legitimizing even the most absurd ideas.

The mind is very easily tricked. In fact, with enough chattering persuasion from that inner voice, the mind will believe anything is real. As Maxwell Maltz pointed out in his seminal book *Psycho Cybernetics*, the mind can be tricked into believing things exist when they don't. All it needs is constant repetition. The mind actually can't tell the difference between something learned from sustained repetition and an actual memory. Powerful shit right?!

This fact can be both good and bad. If you let unfiltered Hate run rampant in your mind 24/7, you'll believe every word it says. If you stop it at every turn, you have a chance.

Hate is not smart. It's instinctual and predictable. Powerful if fed, but powerless if controlled.

So let's look at some of the excuses Hate uses to stop you from making things.

Not enough time

The only truth about not having enough time in the day is that we all have the same amount of time. Anything else is a story concocted by Hate in an effort to prevent you from creating.

This was one of the responses in the group I mentioned earlier:

> "I always wanted to start an online or offline business, but I found out that after a while my focus goes elsewhere. I don't blame my kids, but, with a family, I have very little free time."

This is true. Raising kids is extraordinarily challenging, as are many other life demands. Here are a few other truths you can think of whenever Hate insists you don't have enough time:

1. We all have the same amount of time in a day (even Beyonce!).

2. If you are living in a free country, all time is 'free' and you make the decision how to allocate that time. As a father of two amazing children, I made the decision to allocate a lot of my time to them. I probably don't watch as much TV as the average person, but I do use my 'free' time to run three businesses, outside of writing books and speaking at conferences. All time is free — you choose how to allocate it.

3. Most of our creative output happens when we aren't working. Much like how a bodybuilder's muscles grow during the 21 hours of rest between workouts, it's during the not working that the work actually happens. This is why you get your best ideas when you are relaxed, when you have a change of scenery or are on holidays. Or even when you're in the shower!

4. Research has shown that elite performers don't necessarily spend more time practicing. They are just more productive when they do practice. Learn how to use your time more productively to free up time for making things. There are a bunch of productivity tools and techniques available that the vast majority of people don't use. Things like single-tasking, smaller projects, tracking your progress, setting goals, doing timed work sessions free of interruption, and adding accountability are all proven methods for maximizing your productivity in a short amount of time.

5. When you have less time, you become more productive. It's often then that you really start to see where your priorities lie. When I do my 7 Day Startup Challenges, I really notice this. I do live calls for an hour or so each day and I constantly manage the Facebook group. I run three businesses, and — on top of that — I always set myself a goal for the challenge so I'm 'walking the walk' and participating with the members. On the last challenge, I wrote the last 10,000 words of this book on day 6. It's amazing how effective I can be and how much less time I spend on Facebook and Snapchat when the challenge is running.

Being focused and productive helps weed out the 'I'm time challenged' excuse and gets you an early one-up on Hate.

At this point, you may come to the surprising realization that you actually have too much time, which can make it hard to work out your priorities. This is the exact opposite of what Hate is telling you, which is that you don't have enough time. Work smarter, prioritize, and you'll be on the road to beating Hate by creating more.

Remember, productivity breeds creativity.

If you have less time than most people, consider yourself blessed and get back to work. You have the impetus to become more productive, and therefore more creative.

Failure = course correction

People have a very warped understanding of failure. In *Psycho Cybernetics*, Maxwell Maltz breaks down how humans learn:

> Skill learning of any kind is accomplished by trial and error, mentally correcting aim after an error, until a "successful" motion, movement or performance has been achieved. After that, further learning, and continued success, is accomplished by forgetting the past 'errors,' and remembering the successful response, so that it can be imitated.

Hate will have you think about failure as a fate worse than death. But failure is just course correction. You know where you want to go but you haven't learned how to get there yet. You head towards your goal, stumble, correct course, and keep moving forward.

If you aren't regularly failing, you aren't seeking a new destination. You are following a predictable path that doesn't lead to anything new and you are learning nothing. You aren't creating anything either. In other words, you are failing. You are failing to grow and failing to improve and failing to realize your full potential.

The safe path — the one which you don't have to correct course — is the ultimate failure. This is one of Hate's most powerful tricks. It can make you fail, while making you feel like you are succeeding.

If things are not working, and the failures result in learning and course correction, then failing is a good thing.

If you can fail quickly and without worry, you can correct course quicker, improve quicker, learn more, and achieve more.

If 'things aren't working' is a good thing, then 'this might not work' is a ridiculous reason not to try. In the words of visionary inventor and entrepreneur Elon Musk, "If things are not failing you are not innovating enough."

Another way this manifests is in the excuse of 'I can't see the Return on Investment (ROI)'. People don't take chances unless they are certain of the outcome. But rarely does anything worth doing creatively have a guaranteed outcome.

If things might not work, you are in the realm of uncertainty, which means you are on the right track. If you can't see the ROI, you are on the right track.

I like to aim for a 97% failure rate. When software entrepreneurs start businesses, they aim to give away their product for free and hope 3% of their audience will sign up for the paid version. Obviously they want *all* their free customers to sign up for the paid plan, but they settle for a 97% failure rate.

This ratio has served me well. When I started my mastermind group, I had 7,000 members in the free 7 Day Startup group. I aimed to fail at 97% and have 3% sign up for my paid mastermind.

I had 200 people sign up, which was around 3%. This alone guaranteed more income each year than I'd earned for any of my first 7 years as an entrepreneur.

Failing never felt so good. Aim to fail at 97% or better, and you will be on par with the world's smartest and most successful people.

Hate will have you see a 97% chance of failure as a reason not to try. Creators will use it as a motivator to start now and get to work.

You suck

Hate's ultimate weapon is to incapacitate you by convincing you that you aren't good enough. If you think you aren't good enough, then you won't even bother trying. Hate will tell you that you have no right to try because of how much you suck.

"Knowing I will definitely suck at the first try doesn't help, and that could be my #1 reason for not starting at all." 7 Day Startup Group Member

If you listen to this, Hate can turn these crazy ideas into reality. Instead of allowing that, here are a few things I use to fight it off:

- Steve Jobs said, "...everything around you that you call life was made up by people that were no smarter than you." This is a great quote from one of the most influential creators of our generation, and it's something you can remember any time Hate says, "You aren't good enough!"

- If you are telling yourself you suck, then what you are really saying is that you suck compared to someone else. Comparison is a major creativity killer. If you compare and think you suck, you'll get depressed and give up. If you don't compare yourself with others, you can't suck.

- We are never 100% responsible for our successes or our failures. Keep this in mind if you think you suck because of past failures. The failure might have absolutely nothing to do with you, and someone else's apparent success might have nothing to do with their own efforts.

If Hate is telling you that you suck, just take a step back and think: do you actually suck? Probably not, so let's just move on. If you do, then we can fix that too. More on that later.

You should be doing X

Another trick Hate will pull is trying to convince you that you should be doing something other than creating.

One of the ways Hate presents this is via guilt.

"With kids and other commitments, I feel guilty spending time on it."

Using your kids against you is a Hateful trick. Anyone with kids knows that there's literally nothing on earth that will motivate you more than your kids. So using kids as an excuse can be one of Hate's most cunning and aggressive tricks.

But it's flawed.

As humans, we are poor versions of ourselves when we spend our time doing things we don't want to do. It's the ultimate success hack. Do more of what you love and you will be more successful.

If you let guilt trick you into doing less of what you love, the outcome will be doing a very poor version of whatever guilt has you doing. You will be a poor parent if you spend extra time with your kids only because of guilt.

It's too hard

Feeling overwhelmed is another effective tactic that Hate uses to stop you from making things. If you feel like things are too hard, you will be paralyzed into doing nothing.

The thing you need to remember about achieving anything significant, is that the biggest reason for failure is not starting. We procrastinate on big projects because we can only see the hard parts, so we don't even start.

If you realize this, you realize that it's not the hard parts of the task that are the problem. The problem is the start. Once you start, you are OK.

So, start.

It's probably been done

In the entrepreneurial world, Hate has a very effective trick.

When entrepreneurs think up new ideas, Hate convinces them that someone else has probably done it before. This hateful objection is infectious, as other entrepreneurs will tend to repeat it over and over.

They are laboring under a misguided view that it's only the first to market that succeeds. In reality, this is often not the case. The biggest challenge in business isn't having the best idea, it's commanding the most attention. If you can get more attention for your idea than your competitors, you will win.

Put another way, French author André Gide once said, "Everything that needs to be said has already been said. But since no one was listening, everything must be said again."

Doing things that have already been done might just be a smart way to go. If it's been done, then it means the idea is probably sound. You can then focus on the more important component of drawing attention to the idea.

We are all constantly adapting ideas from other people and putting our own spin on them. It's central to the creative process, and it's a good thing! Austin Kleon, in his book, *Steal Like an Artist*, puts it this way: "What a good artist understands is that nothing comes from nowhere. All creative work builds on what came before. Nothing is completely original."

Stop thinking that what you are doing needs to be a completely original work of art. All anyone does is adapt what people have done before. If it's already been done, good. Do it again, and do it better.

Permission seeking

It's always amazed me in life how much attention people give to the opinions of people who aren't qualified to have one. The quote "lions don't lose sleep over the opinions of sheep" comes to mind.

In my entrepreneurship group, I regularly see people desperately seeking opinions from their peers, or other influencers. It doesn't make sense to post your top three logo designs to Facebook and decide on the top one based on the feedback of people who know nothing about design. It doesn't make sense to ask an influencer what to do in your business, when they know nothing about your business.

What they are really seeking is approval, or permission.

You don't need approval. You don't need permission. You aren't a child anymore.

ZERO TOLERANCE FOR NEGATIVITY

"Negativity is the enemy of creativity."

—David Lynch

Negativity is Hate's currency.

Hate feeds, grows, and spreads on the smallest amount. As we've learned, negativity is the enemy of creation. Having zero tolerance for negativity, and a sharp negativity radar is the solution.

It has been suggested that we are all the average of our five closest friends, so if you choose to accept negativity in people, you will become like them and Hate will thrive.

Here are some things you can do to avoid negativity in other people:

1. Stop being friends with negative people. If you want, you can explain it and see if they are open to change, but they probably won't be. It's your life, and the negativity is eating away at it. You can find new friends.

2. Spend less time with negative family members. When you catch up with them, pay attention to the negativity and have a bit of a laugh about it afterwards. Don't dwell

on it yourself, because dwelling will create negative feelings within you and Hate will creep in.

3. Leave any groups that are dominated by negative people. Often it will only take one or two people to direct the overall feel of the group into negative territory. Most people don't have a good negativity radar, so they don't even see it happening.

4. Avoid friending negative people on social media. I accept most friend requests on my Facebook page, but if I figure out that they are constantly whinging and being negative, I unfriend them. If they are negative on my page, I delete their comments and block them. It's my page, and I never gave them permission to bring their Hate to the party. If they want to Hate, they can do it on their own page. You don't need to give people the opportunity to provide a negative opinion.

5. Over time, people will realize that you don't tolerate negativity and will jump to your aid when it rears its ugly head. Once people realize you have a strong negativity radar, you will improve other people's radars as well.

6. If you feel you can influence other people or other groups into changing, then feel free to try. But don't be disheartened when it doesn't work. It's very difficult to change other people. Be prepared to cut your losses.

Here are some things you can do to avoid negativity in yourself:

- Completely eliminate negative self-talk. This is the root of all internal negativity and as we've learned, it's a self-fulfilling prophecy. If you tell yourself you are shit, you will be shit.

- Realize that negativity is boring and people don't actually care. If you are the one who is always whinging about how hard things are and how much you are struggling, people probably won't like you. As Dale Carnegie pointed out in *How to Win Friends and Influence People*, "Talk to someone about themselves and they'll listen for hours." Talk about yourself for hours, and people will tune you out.

- Listen to yourself next time you are communicating online or in person. Are you being negative about what is going on? Are you listening to what the other person has to say? Or are you only talking about yourself and your so-called 'problems'?

- If you are openly negative towards others, people will dislike you. They won't tell you, and probably won't make it obvious. (I will, but most people won't.) People want to be loved and appreciated, and they want to feel like they are valuable. Negativity will do the opposite.

Without knowing why, they will start to resent you.

- Practice self-awareness, gratitude, and empathy on a regular basis.

Staying positive isn't easy for everybody. It's something I have to constantly work on and you might have to as well. For others it comes naturally, but it still helps to cultivate a negativity radar, so you can see it in other people and stop it in its tracks.

CULTIVATING SELF-AWARENESS

"Your visions will become clear only when you can look into your own heart. Who looks outside, dreams; who looks inside, awakes."

—C.G. Jung

Self-awareness is the key to recognizing and managing Hate.

Whether it's determining if negativity is taking over, discovering a new ability, or working on gratitude and empathy, at some point you need to look at yourself and determine how well you are doing. People probably won't tell you.

Understanding yourself and being honest with yourself are two of the most beneficial skills in life, and they will directly help you reduce Hate and boost creativity.

Here are a few things that help to cultivate a healthy level of self awareness:

1. Personality quizzes such as a DiSC Profile, Myers-Briggs types, or the Yohari Window are a good place to start. Don't let them pigeonhole you into being a certain type of person, though. Use them to help you understand yourself better. For example, you might use them to figure out why you like or dislike certain things or situations.

2. Avoid assumptions wherever possible, and look for the data. After a string of failed businesses, I learned not to back my own great ideas too heavily. Sure, I still launch ideas when I get them, but I do it quickly and get it in the hands of customers as soon as possible. That way, I don't have to rely on my assumptions and can look at the real external data to determine if it's really such an epic idea after all. If you want to know what you are good at, try a lot of things and see what people appreciate with their actions, not just their words.

3. Fail a lot. The more things you try that don't work, the closer you will get to something that does work. Learn from your failures, and keep swinging.

4. Get better at reading between the lines. People around you will rarely tell you the truth, particularly if they love you. I notice this is especially true for people who are particularly focused on being positive all the time. It's great to be positive, but when you want critical feedback, positive people can be a lot harder to read. Self awareness is critical, and if you do need feedback from others, you need to read between the lines and look at body language and facial expressions, instead of the words they use. My girlfriend Emma is always super positive about absolutely anything I do. It's great, but it's not that useful if I want to know whether my work is good or bad, be-

cause she always says it's good! But I've learned to read between the lines. "Yeah it's great, you might want to change this," means that it is not very good. If it really was great, she'd say, "far out, that's epic!"

Get better at knowing yourself — not in a judgemental way, but in a real way that's in touch with your true self.

If you notice you're being negative, it's OK to say to yourself, "I'm being negative now, I'm helping Hate, so just stop it." It's not OK to say, "I'm so negative." That's training your mind to believe that you are a negative person, and before long, you will believe it.

BE MORE GRATEFUL, BE MORE CREATIVE

"Acknowledging the good that you already have in your life is the foundation for all abundance."

—Eckhart Tolle

A lot of Hate stems from a lack of gratitude. Having a lack of gratitude will lead directly to negativity, which is the currency of Hate. If you can become more grateful, you will become less hateful and, therefore, more creative.

Gratitude also kills anger and stress. It's very hard to be grateful and angry at the same time, which means gratitude directly increases relaxation — the state where creativity thrives. We'll talk more about relaxation in a bit.

When people complain about something someone has made, it's often that they are simply not grateful enough for the amount of time and effort that went into making it. You can still display gratitude for the time and effort spent creating something, without having to like or buy the end product itself.

Before you start whinging about the $5 you just paid for your coffee, consider what has gone into it.

Seeds are planted (in the perfect environment), the seed-lings are replanted into individual pots, watered regularly and shaded from bright sunlight before being re-planted in soil. Three to four years later, the trees bear fruit known as cherries. These are generally hand-picked by people, often in poorer countries, who pick 100-200 cherries a day and are paid based on their haul.

The cherries are processed using a complicated, mostly manual method of wet or dry processing. The beans are hulled, polished, graded, and sorted before being packaged and loaded onto ships for export. The beans are then roasted locally, an expensive process to bring out the oils that deliver the coffee flavour. They are then transported to coffee shops, ground on-site, expertly brewed and delivered to you hot and fresh by well-paid local staff, in a matter of minutes. $5 doesn't really seem like such a big deal now, does it?

Here are some other practical ways to become more grateful:

- A daily gratitude practice might be all you need. Just list off a few things you are grateful for each day and why. Imagine life without the most basic things you take for granted, and say to yourself, I'm grateful for x because of y. A gratitude journal, a note taking app, notebook, or even just saying them out loud can work.

- It also helps to notice when others aren't being grateful, so you can get constant reminders of the importance of gratitude. I have zero tolerance for ungrateful people. I can spot it a mile away, which makes it much easier to spot in myself.

- James Altucher talks about attacking a 'Difficult Gratitude Problem,' or DGP as I now call it. Like a muscle, gratitude gets stronger when you train it on challenges rather than the obvious stuff. So, let difficult circumstances trigger gratitude. If you step in dog shit, just remember DGP and start thinking about all the wonderful things that result from dogs. If you can be grateful about stepping in shit, you are doing well!

- Variety can also be a great driver of gratitude. I find living by the beach helps with gratitude, because it always looks and smells different; it forces me to take notice. If you can build variety into your life through your routine or with travel, or if you can work on becoming more observant to variety around you, you will have more gratitude.

- Another trick that works well is catching yourself saying, 'I *have* to do *x*,' and changing it to, 'I *get* to do *x*.' Most of us don't really have to do anything; we choose to do it. More often than not, when you think about the choices you are making, you will feel good about the opportunities you have every day.

- Helping out people who are less fortunate can make you realize how fortunate you are.

- Take a week off complaining, or at least a day. Every time you find yourself complaining about anything, stop and move on. You will be forced to think about something differently and you'll break the negative thinking pattern.

- Some people like watching the news to remind themselves to be grateful for their own life. I personally don't ever watch the news, because it's filled with too much fear and negativity, and I don't want that creeping into my mind. But do what works for you.

Be more grateful, be more creative.

EMPATHY BREEDS CREATIVITY

"*Writing is a sustained act of empathy.*"

—Andre Dubois

Empathy is another way to kill negativity. Because most of us are fundamentally self-interested, we oversimplify things and undervalue them.

In the coffee example, we think, "this coffee is too expensive for me." But we don't really know what it's like to be the person picking the cherries for 10 hours every day, taking them up to the weighing station, and hoping they made enough money for their family. We can't feel what it's like to be the person working on the ship, at sea for weeks, bringing the container over. We didn't wake up at 5am to run a coffee shop business where we probably earn half of what we are worth and work double the hours.

We don't have enough empathy to understand what it's like to be someone else.

Becoming a more empathic person makes you more understanding, more grateful, less negative, and therefore more creative.

The secret to empathy is not imagining what it's like to be in someone else's shoes. Because all that does is put *you* in *their* shoes. It's *them* in their shoes we need to understand, not *you* in their shoes.

When you prescribe simple solutions to people's problems, that's mistakenly putting yourself in someone else's shoes.

For example, when someone is overweight, a typical response to the situation may be to think: "just exercise more and stop eating McDonalds!" Because that's what you would do.

But that person is not you. They might have had a lifetime of being put down; they might have low or non-existent self-esteem; they might not even understand the value of healthy food; they might have tried to join the gym 10 times and failed every time. You don't really know their circumstances, but you assume you know their situation, because we assume everyone is like us.

You need to first accept that you really don't know what it's like to be someone other than yourself. Once you accept that, you won't be as quick to judge. You will be more likely to listen and observe and try to understand people better.

Empathy is an extremely difficult skill to master because no one lives inside someone else's body and mind. But there are things you can do to improve it:

1. Start from this simple place: You are a self-interested human being. Everything you see, you apply your own context to. But everyone else is also self-interested, and they apply their context to everything. Admit that: "I actually don't understand anyone unless I make an attempt to understand them."

2. Don't rush into responses and don't rush to judgement.

3. The next time you see someone driving fast, don't be so quick to assume you know everything about that person and why they are doing it. If you can judge people less, you can understand people better.

4. Notice empathy in others. Most people don't have a lot of empathy, but some people do. If you can notice it when you see it, you are more likely to improve your own skills. Notice people who are curious, who don't just talk about themselves but eagerly want to hear about others.

5. Spend more time in person with friends, customers, and business colleagues. It's very easy to make snap judgements online and forget about the people behind the status updates. Spending more time in person cuts through it all and helps you to remember and really understand the individual.

6. Don't talk as much. During a conversation, listen more and ask open questions. People will fill in the gaps with their own words, and you'll learn more about them and focus less on yourself.

7. Create more things. It's very easy to judge someone else for something they made if you don't ever create anything for yourself. The more you create, the more you will understand what people go through while putting their ideas out into the world. Ultimately, you'll be less quick to judge.

8. Realize that empathy and sympathy are not the same thing. Saying, "oh, you poor thing," doesn't make someone feel like they've been heard. Instead, take your time and really try to understand how it might feel to be that person. Sympathy could even make it worse. Avoid amplifying the grief of others by dwelling on their suffering. They don't want grief; they didn't ask for it. It's not about you.

9. Being overly optimistic can actually hurt empathy. If you are feeling down about something, and your loved ones are just saying, "it's great, you are awesome", the outcome can be the opposite to what was intended. It will make you feel like the person isn't really understanding, and it will kill communication. If a person is down about something, pretending everything is amazing is the opposite of empathy. It doesn't mean dwelling on their negativity, it just means listening.

10. The next time you are in a conversation, stop yourself from talking unless you absolutely have to. Not inter-

rupting will help you understand what it's like to go into a conversation with no agenda and with your full attention on actually listening to the other person. Don't make any sympathetic noises such as 'ooooh' or 'yeah' or 'right' (another reason in person conversations are best). Instead, just ask the occasional question if the silence is unbearable. Empathy is about listening. The more you talk, the less you are listening.

11. Learn to become a better listener and communicator. Reading books on communication or doing training in communication will make you notice when you are acting with judgement as opposed to empathy.

12. What about the idea of Difficult Empathy Problems (DEP)? Don't just feel empathy for people who are very much like you. What if you challenged yourself to feel empathy for people who you really struggle to understand? What about feeling empathy for people filled with hate?

13. Practice reading other people's emotions. What do you notice about their body language, their speed of talking, their eyes, their words? The more you can understand how people express emotions, the more you will understand other people.

If you are an entrepreneur, empathy is your business.

Empathy is not only one of the most valuable life skills, it's also one of the most valuable business and marketing skills. Poor business people present their offer to customers as if they are speaking to themselves. Great marketers have deep empathy for the customer, and a true understanding of who they are, what they feel, how they speak, what they care about, and what drives them. This enables them to speak to their customers in a way that is more likely to result in sales.

This is why businesses pay copywriters to write their sales materials, because most business owners don't have enough empathy. Copywriters know that the secret to great copy is to have deep empathy.

But the coolest thing to remember is that empathy is about imagination. Your goal in being empathic is to imagine what it's like to be that person and feel what they are feeling. If you can improve your empathy, you improve your imagination. And imagination is the source of all creativity.

See? Empathy breeds creativity.

AM I GOOD ENOUGH?

"Competence leads to confidence."

—Dan Norris

One of the biggest reasons people don't make things is because they let Hate convince them that they aren't good enough. We already talked about this under 'Disarming Hate,' where we recognized the belief in one's own incompetence as just an excuse.

Perfectionism is another trick Hate will use to stop you from making things. If Hate can convince you that everything has to be perfect, it knows you won't begin, or at least that you won't finish the task you are striving to complete.

Have you ever heard the saying "Done is better than perfect"? Whenever I used to hear this saying I thought, "That's a cute quote, but let's be real. Perfect is always better!"

It took me a while to get it. There is no such thing as perfect, which is why 'Done' is better. Because often the choice ends up being 'Done' or 'Nothing'. And 'Done' wins, every time. Therefore, do more.

It is possible, though, that you actually aren't good enough.

Do you have to be good?

If you feel like you aren't good enough, the first thing to think about is whether or not you have to be good.

For example, if you are creating something just for fun, it really doesn't matter if you are good. If you sing because you want to be a musician, you have to be a good singer. If you get drunk and go to Karaoke, it doesn't really matter how good you are.

Even professionally, some areas are more tolerant than others when it comes to not being the world's best. Most business people who speak at events aren't good public speakers. They make all the mistakes you learn about in a one-day speaker training course. You don't have to be Tony Robbins to speak at a business event.

The same is true with writing. You can write a great business book even if you aren't a great writer. If you have a good story, or an interesting idea, you can get away with not being Shakespeare.

No matter what you do, it always helps to be as good as you can be. But you don't always have to be the best in the world to do something successfully.

Get good enough

The alternative, if you are self-aware enough to realize you aren't as good as you need to be, is to get better.

There have been times in my life when I wasn't confident in what I was making. One of those times was when I first started building websites for companies. I left my well-paying government job at 26, with literally no website development experience or qualifications, and started a web design business. I'd never built a single website for anyone before.

I told companies I could build their websites for them, but it didn't feel right. I didn't feel like I was very good at it. Guess what? I was right!

So I got better. I bought books on programming, I paid my friends to teach me design, I built a bunch of sites for myself, and eventually I figured out how to make decent websites. Then I got into more advanced sites, like e-commerce stores and online learning portals, and started offering things my competitors couldn't offer.

I got a lot more confident in what I was doing, and that gave me the confidence to make more things.

Do something else

If you really feel like you can't be good at something, and you are really honest with yourself, you can do something else.

The idea that changing something is giving up or failing is crazy.

If you decide to correct your course towards something new that feels right, then good for you. It's important to feel like you are doing great work, which will result in more creative output.

My turning point came when I gave up on my web design business of seven years and started from scratch. It felt like I was letting myself down at the time; I had persisted until it almost killed me, only to give up and go back to square one. It was a devastating process, but it didn't have to be. All I was doing was course-correcting, and in hindsight I wish I had done it five years earlier.

When I started again, my motivation went through the roof and my creative output soared. It hasn't relented since.

SHUT THE FUCK UP AND ENJOY THE GREATNESS

"It takes a healthy ego to get up in the morning and say, 'I deserve to be here.'"

—Peter Riegert

When you are someone who makes things, there comes a time when you just get sick of your own Hate, and the Hate of others trying to stop you from making things.

This is the time for a healthy ego to do its thing.

Kanye West is a guy I've looked up to for a long time as an example of someone who makes things. He's had his "I'm a gigantic cock" moments for sure, but with a bit of empathy, you can understand what it must be like to live with all the negative attention he gets.

What I have noticed about Kanye is that he keeps creating things. Most people with that level of public attention don't. Kanye will often, and quite drastically, change his music style from album to album. He also makes clothes that are enormously popular. Occasionally he makes an arse of himself, which is always entertaining, and from time to time he makes tweets. This one caught my eye:

"SHUT THE FUCK UP AND ENJOY THE GREATNESS."

There are a lot of people who just criticize what other people make. They have lost the battle with Hate and Hate is now in control.

Don't blame them, just tell them to shut the fuck up and enjoy the greatness. Whether you tweet it out in all caps, or just whisper it to yourself as a reminder, is your call.

CHAPTER 4

HOW TO BE CREATIVE

You know you are creative, but that doesn't mean you spend enough of your time being creative. You have it in you, but it doesn't come out often enough.

A quote by Russell Brand, talking on the *Joe Rogan Experience* podcast, springs to mind: "There's no viagra for enlightenment."

There's no one simple solution to solve or overcome problems that mankind has faced since the dawn of time. Intellectual and moral enlightenment is a complex process of learning and improvement that never ends.

Your creativity is the same. There is no magic bullet that will kill Hate off for good. Instead, you need to constantly practice creating more. You can't just become creative or be creative indefinitely.

Let's look at some ways you can go about being creative and making more things.

FOLLOW YOUR FLOW

"It is when we act freely, for the sake of the action itself rather than for ulterior motives, that we learn to become more than what we were."

—Mihaly Csikszentmihalyi

A common piece of advice in entrepreneurship circles is that the key to success is to simply follow your passion. This advice is very easy to misinterpret.

When I was a desperate failure, trying to figure out what business to start, I fell into this trap.

Passion is a powerful idea, which isn't typically associated with intensive labor.

When I thought about my passion, the only thing that came close was surfing. I love surfing, it seemed like a cool industry to be involved with, and I had an idea that I thought could work. An app that lets surfers check in on their surf breaks and leave a review. Great idea! Gnarly, dude, I'm following my passion!

The problem was, no one wanted to pay for that, and it was too hard for me to see a situation where advertisers would be interested enough to give me money. The other problem was that building an app for surfers didn't have me surfing any more than I did previously. If following your passion means you're not getting to indulge your passion any more than before, then what's the point?

In his excellent book *Show Your Work*, renowned creative Austin Kleon explains it this way:

> "When a painter talks about her 'work', she could be talking about two different things: There's the artwork, the finished piece,… and there's the art 'work'. All the day-to-day stuff that goes on behind the scenes in her studio."

If you are passionate about showing off pieces of art, but not about spending all day every day slaving over the canvas, then it's probably not the best idea to start an art business.

In my case, I do like surfing and as far as passions go it's a pretty good one. But there was something else I noticed about my work days. I hated most of the work time I spent building websites for people, but I loved every chance I got to write blog posts.

Very few people were reading them, but it was just about the only thing I did on a regular basis that made me feel like time was flying by. I had stayed up a few nights writing blog posts, barely noticing time pass as I churned out thousands of words. The psychologist Mihaly Csikszentmihalyi refers to this as a state of flow.

"In positive psychology, flow, also known as the zone, is the mental state of operation in which a person performing an activity is fully immersed in a feeling of energized focused involvement and enjoyment throughout the activity. In essence, flow is characterized by complete absorption in what one does."

I would never say I'm passionate about writing blog posts. I've never attended a writing conference, never studied or trained to be a writer, and I barely even talk to my friends about writing. I don't even consider myself to be a writer, even though I've written 4 books and hundreds of posts and articles.

But the state of flow that occurred when I wrote gave me a clue about what I really wanted to be doing.

I recognized this, and decided to build a business where my day-to-day activity would be writing blog posts to draw attention to my business.

Following your passion puts too much pressure on you to take what you love and somehow turn it into something epic and sexy that other people will understand and latch onto. It makes you think about the final result, not the day-to-day work required to make it happen. The things you're passionate about excite you so much they give you chills.

But success isn't built on chills. It's built on constantly making things.

If there's something you can do that has you making things without you even noticing the work, then I'd say that's a good start!

Follow your flow.

CREATE MORE THAN YOU CONSUME

*"Success usually comes to those who are
too busy to be looking for it."*

—Henry David Thoreau

Understand that you have two choices: to create something or consume something.

Most people just consume things. They watch TV, read books and blog posts, complete training, and refine their craft. They spend so much time consuming that they have no time left for creating. In the business world, we call this being addicted to entrepornography.

If you want to be an actively creative person, you have to create more than you consume.

If you read two hours a day, that's great! But if you don't then write for more than two hours, you will have fallen into the trap of consuming more than you create.

Look at how much you are consuming versus what you are creating, and try to match them up. Remember, starting is the hardest part. Once you begin creating, you will find it much easier to create more.

Most people find this with writing — once they start, they can write forever.

CREATE SO MUCH THEY CAN'T IGNORE YOU

*"If you hear a voice within you say you cannot paint,
then by all means paint and that voice will be silenced."*

—Vincent van Gogh

Steve Martin has a great quote, "Be so good they can't ignore you." I love this because it puts the responsibility squarely back in your court. It's your job to be good; the rest will look after itself. If you really are that good, people will eventually notice.

The problem is, in the public sphere, it's up to others to decide if you are good enough. When you make things, aiming for that 97% failure rate, it is virtually guaranteed that whatever you make won't be good enough for most people.

With this in mind, I made up my own version of Martin's quote:

Create so much they can't ignore you.

Making stuff is entirely up to you. It doesn't matter if it's a hit. It only matters that you made it. This knowledge has served me well, and it's the only reason I've been able to do what I do.

I wrote 300 blog posts before I had one with more than 10 shares. I know people who got hundreds of shares on their first blog post. Good for them. I'm going to keep writing blog posts.

Steven Pressfield — the successful author of numerous works of historical fiction and screenplays — wrote for 17 years before getting his first book deal. If it's good enough for one of the most prolific writers of our generation, it's good enough for me.

This is my fourth book, despite never having been offered a publishing deal. I have friends who are first-time authors who were given multiple six-figure deals for their first book. I'm happy for them. I'm going to keep making books.

I've posted almost 4,000 images on Instagram and have less than 7,000 followers. My girlfriend has posted less and has almost 70,000 followers. My friend Nathan has posted less than both of us and has 700,000 followers. Kim Kardashian has posted less and has 70,000,000 followers.

That's great for them. As for me, I'm going to keep posting what I believe is good content until my account gets noticed. If it doesn't, I'm going to keep creating content on another platform until that gets noticed. I'm going to enjoy the process of creating things on all the great platforms I have the privilege to use.

Taking this approach doesn't mean blindly putting out crap in the hope that one day something will stick. It's your job to make sure you make good stuff.

But the world is filled with good stuff. Which means you might create good stuff 5,000 times before anyone notices. If you want to get noticed, you might need to create 5,001 things.

BREAK IT DOWN

"When eating an elephant take one bite at a time."

—Creighton Abrams

In *Steal Like an Artist*, Austin Kleon suggests reducing your options in order to make the task of creating much simpler. He argues that "when it comes to creative work, limitations mean freedom." Starting a business with no money, for example, forces you to be more creative with your marketing.

Reducing the scope can also reduce the friction that accompanies the beginning of any project, which is the biggest problem we have to overcome. If the job is easier, you are more likely to do it. On larger projects, people visualize the most difficult parts of the project and Hate creeps in to scare them away.

Make your creative projects simpler, and you'll be more likely to start.

I did that with this book by making it only exist for one reason: to help you create something today. I decided it should be a lot smaller and shorter than my other books. The first draft took me three days to write, and the book was released a few months after I had the idea.

If you can't reduce the scope of the project, you can break

it down into smaller chunks. I do this with all of my writing because it helps me stay motivated to complete the project. As someone who was never good at English and never saw myself as a good writer, I'm pretty amazed that I was able to write one book, let alone four books in four years!

But I shouldn't be, because a book is really only 15 blog posts. I routinely write 2,000 word blog posts, so I know I can write a 2,000 word chapter. Fifteen chapters at 2,000 words is 30,000 words, which is the length of my first book, *The 7 Day Startup.*

I never thought I would be able to write a book until I wrote down all the things I wanted to talk about and started checking them off a list as I wrote the words.

With that book and every book since, I start with a Google Doc and at the top of the document I summarize my progress. I write out the chapter headings, guessing as best I can what they will be, and I add a count of how many words I've written next to each one. At the end of each writing session, I note an overall percentage of completion based on either the word count or the number of chapters.

This book was no different. Here is an example of what I included at the top of the draft as I was writing it:

12,567 words

21 / 28 (75%)

(Numbers are a snapshot from one point in the process)

It motivates me every step of the way. In the first two hours I spent on the project, I'd written three chapters and passed 10% completion.

There's a lot more to a book than the first draft, but I know that if I can write a whole book I will be able to release it. So I don't think about perfecting the book, editing it, designing it, formatting it, publishing it or marketing it. I know all of that stuff will happen if I just write it.

All I concern myself with is how far I've progressed with that task.

RELAXATION → CREATIVITY

"Forget about being an expert or a professional, and wear your amateurism (your heart, your love) on your sleeve."

—Austin Kleon

Most of our creative effort happens when we're not working. Relaxation is the key to unleashing the power of creativity.

Here's what Maxwell Maltz says in *Psycho Cybernetics* about relaxation and its relationship to the mechanism by which we create and achieve things:

> Physical relaxation, when practiced daily, brings about an accompanying 'mental relaxation' and a 'relaxed attitude', which enables us to better consciously control our automatic mechanism. Physical relaxation also, in itself, has a powerful influence in de-hypnotizing us from negative attitudes and reaction patterns.

One of the big challenges of creativity is the ability to disempower Hate, which is often an instinctual and automated reaction, and embrace our creativity with more controlled emotions like empathy and gratitude.

Relaxation gives us the ability to do this.

It's impossible to control your emotions when you are stressed. Reduce the pressure on yourself, reduce stress, and learn to relax. Meditate daily if you want, go on a holiday, surf, go for a walk, or take a shower. Do whatever you need to do to relax, and your creative juices will flow.

Stanford researchers found that going for a walk can improve creativity by as much as 60%.

Scott Barry Kaufman, Ph.D., a cognitive psychologist and creativity expert, found that 72% of people experience new ideas in the shower. He commented: "people are more creative in the shower than they are at work. The relaxing, solitary, and non-judgmental shower environment may afford creative thinking by allowing the mind to wander freely, causing people to be more open to their inner stream of consciousness and daydreams."

Interestingly, Austin Kleon and Elizabeth Gilbert both advocate undertaking your creative projects as hobbies before making a living with them. As hobbies, you have less stress and there's less on the line, enabling you to relax and free up your creativity.

FEED YOUR CREATIVITY

*"Every child is an artist, the problem is staying
an artist when you grow up."*

—Pablo Picasso

In order for your creativity to thrive, you need to feed it.

I like to surround myself with positive friends, run groups of creative people on Facebook, listen to positive people on podcasts, and follow quote accounts on Instagram. All of this helps to constantly feed my creativity.

Do what works for you. Again, with self-awareness, you'll discover what YOU need to stay in the creative mindset. You might like documentaries, you might love reading books. Don't fall into the trap of consuming more than you create, but consume as much as you need to help your creativity thrive.

Rather than just absorbing information and inspiration, collect your ideas in a note-taking app and revisit them regularly. Seeing all the ideas listed out will feed your creativity further, as you'll have lots of things to explore.

Broaden the sources you use to inspire yourself.

Don't just surround yourself with the same people from the same cliquey groups. If you are an entrepreneur, study design and architecture. If you are a writer, study film or art. The point isn't acquiring new skills, the point is fueling your creativity by immersing yourself in other forms of creativity.

Build your self-awareness and do more of what works for you.

CHASE SHINY OBJECTS

"With science, there is this culture of experimentation, and most of the time, those experiments fail."

—John Lasseter

As a failed entrepreneur, people used to tell me to stop chasing shiny objects. I stuck at my first business for seven years, failing year after year after year. At least I was focused, right?

Chasing shiny objects is apparently a "syndrome" amongst entrepreneurs, which causes people to spend time pursuing opportunities and trying new things. Sounds like a pretty fun syndrome to me!

I was criticized heavily for chasing shiny things. This is what one of my friends, a fellow entrepreneur, said about me at the time:

You're flaky — you create 'abandon-ware' and haphazardly 'fire' paying customers. In the past few months we've seen you start with one product, add two more and watched them disappear just as fast as they appeared. Now you're working on a completely separate product. Who is going to invest their time in you and your products?

As it turns out, thousands of people wanted to invest time *and* money into my products. This comment came a few weeks before I created my WordPress support business, WP Curve, when I asked for feedback on the idea. That business took off and within two years we had over 1,000 customers, 40 contractors around the world working for us, and over $1m USD per year in annual run rate.

All of a sudden, I was a genius business person.

In two years I'd gone from a diagnosed sufferer of shiny object syndrome to a seven-figure entrepreneur, best-selling author, and international speaker.

Sometimes it takes a while to find your place. I spent 33 years on earth never really being that good at anything, but I kept trying new things and chasing those shiny objects until I found one or two that exploded.

CHANGE SCENERY

*"Travel and change of place impart
new vigor to the mind."*

—Seneca

For whatever reason, I haven't written many of the words in my books at my desk. My first book, *The 7 Day Startup*, I wrote in my backyard on an outdoor table over a few consecutive afternoons. I'd never worked on the table before, but I made that my routine for those few days and the words poured out.

Most of the words in my other books have been written on planes.

There's something about a change of scenery that puts you in the mood to create. For me, being on a plane is the right combination of stimuli. There's no internet and therefore no distractions, I hate flying and sitting still, so I need something to focus on.

The first 12,000 words of my second book, *Content Machine*, were written on a six-hour flight. I wrote 6,000 words for my third book, *Operation Brewery*, when we flew to China to inspect our brewing equipment. The last 10,000 words were written on a flight to the U.S., where I also wrote the first 5,000 words of this book.

I'm not the only person who's formed this curious habit of writing books on planes. My friend, entrepreneur and bestselling business author Peter Shankman, once booked a return flight from the U.S. to Japan to write his book *Zombie Loyalists* when his deadline was approaching!

Maybe it's an ADHD thing, I don't know (Peter also hosts the popular podcast *Faster Than Normal*, about successful people working with different forms of ADHD). But we've found what works for us!

Of course, there are less extreme ways to change scenery, so try a few options and see what works for you. A weekend getaway is a good start, an overseas trip even better.

BUILD YOUR CREATIVE TOOLKIT

"Write while the heat is in you. The writer who postpones the recording of his thoughts uses an iron which has cooled to burn a hole with. He cannot inflame the minds of his audience."

—Henry David Thoreau

Keep ready access to a toolkit that helps you create.

Whether it's notepads and pens, whiteboards or butcher's paper, use what works for you.

I'm a digital guy, so I always have a note-taking app (Google Keep) on my phone for recording ideas. I also have Trello, a post-it note style app, on my phone and Mac for visualizing ideas on a page, categorizing, and planning. I use Google Docs for fleshing out my ideas further, and ultimately turning them into full blown projects.

I've found having a desk with nothing but a laptop on it works well. Reducing the clutter helps me to relax and focus.

Make sure that whether you are in your work space or out and about, you have a creativity toolkit that allows you to spring into action and embrace your creative impulses when they surface.

CREATE WITH OTHERS

*"It is literally true that you can succeed best and
quickest by helping others to succeed."*

—Napoleon Hill

One of the best things I've done in business is to become active in a bunch of online communities. There's nothing like the support of others to help drive your creative output.

I now have my own group on Facebook called "The 7 Day Startup". I run challenges where participants are given 7 days to launch a project or achieve a goal that they set themselves.

People get extremely creative during these challenges. It's an environment where everyone is supporting each other, and it drives them to create more. Participants have used the time and the challenges to launch six-figure businesses, create blogs, create online courses, and write tens of thousands of words for a book.

You can do the same thing in person with your friends. Give it a go and see if it increases your output.

When Snapchat was emerging, I bet my girlfriend Emma that I could beat her and her sister Carla to 500 views on Snapchat. We all got excited and started snapping a lot more. They destroyed me, as expected, and I had to buy them a nice dinner. But we all got pretty good at Snapchat, and started being mentioned on blogs and in groups when the topic of who to follow came up.

We had fun, we created more, and everyone won.

The other advantage to creating with others is the enormous benefit you get personally when you help other people.

At the very least, you'll have the satisfaction of making a positive impact on someone else's creative journey. But I'm willing to bet you will get a lot more out of the experience.

For one thing, you will become less self-interested and more empathic, traits that will directly lead you to be more creative.

Perhaps even more valuable is the additional power you give to your creative side when you help fuel creativity in others. Hate will not survive in an environment where you are directly influencing creative work.

Create with others, help others, and creativity will flourish.

EMBRACE THE MAGIC

"Go for it now. The future is promised to no one."

—Wayne Dyer

I'm not a religious person.

I grew up Catholic with an ex-Christian Brother for a dad. Towards the end of primary school, our waning interest in attending Sunday mass was showing.

There came a point when Dad couldn't fight it anymore. We obviously had no interest in being at church. My older brother paved the way for me, and by the time I was heading to high school, I could skip church almost consequence-free.

I'm not a spiritual person. I don't meditate or do yoga. I drink beer and analyze things, that's me.

But sometimes stuff happens that I could choose to ignore, choose to enjoy, choose to dismiss, or choose to use as creative fuel.

For example, on the day I decided to write this book, an event occurred that I chose to enjoy and use as creative fuel. I posted about writing the book in my Facebook Group and my friend Claire saw it. Later on, when she went to work, she found a business card on her chair, and it said:

Feeling bad: Create

Feeling good: Create

Feeling great: Create

Whether it was a spiritual sign from God, or not, I had a choice to either ignore this coincidence or embrace it. It made me smile, so I saw it as a sign that I was on the right track.

On the plane writing this book, I took a break to read a bit about the topic of creativity. I had recently asked for some suggestions from my Facebook group on what to read. I bought a bunch of their suggestions before the flight and once we were onboard, I picked one that jumped out at me. It was called *Steal Like an Artist*, by Austin Kleon. I read a few chapters then quickly got back to writing this book. (I always prefer to be creating more than consuming).

When we arrived in the U.S., we settled in with our friends, Marleen and Derek, in Ojai, California. When it was my turn for the shower, I went into the bathroom, and sitting on the top of the toilet was the exact same book by Austin Kleon.

Again, not an impossible set of events, but stuff like that was happening a lot! Call it synchronicity, call it magic, or call it confirmation bias. However you want to phrase it, it's enjoyable and motivating.

If you look for it, you might find it yourself, and create more as a result.

Most creative people speak about a force that drives their creativity that's bigger than themselves, and none more emphatically than Wayne Dyer.

On 26 June 2012, Wayne Dwyer, a prolific author, sat his family down and told them he was done writing. He had no interest in writing a memoir — he felt way too young for that.

On 27 June, he woke up and reversed his decision. That day, he started writing *I Can See Clearly Now*, a book about the power of stepping back and appreciating what is taking place in your life. He looked back over his own life in order to teach lessons and help others do the same thing.

He didn't know why he wrote the book, it just came. He wrote for 90 days straight, mornings, afternoons and evenings. He said it was like something took over. Something was moving the pieces. The writing was so smooth and clear that it hardly even needed editing.

He wasn't one to ignore it when the world threw things like this at him. If he felt like making something, he made it.

I Can See Clearly Now was published in 2014, and in August 2015 Wayne Dyer died suddenly of a heart attack.

Do I think it was some kind of spiritual guide or God

pushing him to write one more book? Unlikely. But he was inspired and he embraced it. Over the course of his life, he wrote 42 books, selling 35 million copies.

Cynicism kills creativity. Embrace the magic.

TODAY'S TASK:
MAKE SOMETHING

This was a short book. It's only purpose was to inspire you to make something today.

Go and do it.

I would love to know what you make. Hit me up on social media. My handle is @thedannorris on Instagram, Snapchat, and Twitter. Share your project using the hashtag #createorhate.

My free group is full of creatives who are making things every day. You can join it by going to Facebook and searching for "The 7 Day Startup".

See you in there, and happy creating.

REFERENCES

1. Altucher, J. (2015). Are you the exception or the rule? [Web long post] James Altucher. Retreieved from http://www.jamesaltucher.com/2015/06/are-you-the-exception-or-the-rule/

2. Brand, R. (2016, June 21). Russell Brand & Jim Breuer. [Podcast]. *Joe Rogan podcast*. Retrieved from http://podcasts.joerogan.net/podcasts/russell-brand-jim-breuer

3. Carnegie, D. (1998). *How to win friends and influence people*. New York, NY: Pocket Books.

4. Ciotte, G. (n.d.). The science of productivity. [Web log post] Gregory Ciotte. Retrieved from http://www.sparringmind.com/productivity-science/

5. Dyer, W. (2015). *I can see clearly now*. Carlsbad: Hay House, Inc.

6. Hansgrohe. (2014, April). *Shower for the freshest thinking*. Retrieved from http://www1.hansgrohe.com/assets/at--de/1404_Hansgrohe_Select_ConsumerSurvey_EN.pdf

7. Jobs, S. (2012). *Steve Jobs: secrets of life, timeless words of wisdom*. Silicon Valley Historical Association. 2012. Retrieved from http://www.siliconvalleyhistorical.org/steve-jobs-secrets-of-life-movie

8. Kleon, A. (2012). *Steal like an artist*. New York, NY: Workman Publishing Company, Inc.

9. Kleon, A. (2014). *Show your work*. New York, NY: Workman Publishing Company, Inc.

10. Martin, S. (2007, December 12). *Charlie Rose show*. Charlie Ross LLC. Retrieved from https://charlierose.com/videos/20473

11. Maltz, M. (1960). *Psycho cybernetics*. New York: Prentice-Hall.

12. Musk, E qtd. in Reigngold, J. (2005). Hondas in space. *Fast company*. Retrieved from https://www.fastcompany.com/52065/hondas-space

13. Norris, D. (2014). *The 7 day startup: you don't learn until you launch*. CreateSpace Independent Publishing Platform.

14. Norris, D. (2015). *Content machine: use content marketing to build a 7-figure business with zero advertising*. CreateSpace Independent Publishing Platform

15. Norris, D. (2016). *Operation brewery: black hops - the least covert operation in brewing: a step-by-step guide to building a brewery on a budget*. CreateSpace Independent Publishing Platform.

16. Shankman, P. (2015). *Zombie loyalists: using great service to create rabid fans*. New York: St. Martin's Press LLC.

17. Sutton, R. (2011). "The truth is, creativity isn't about wild talent as much as it's about productivity". In Web Augustine (Ed.), *$500,000* Worth of Inspiring Quotations for Our Times* (p. 50). Zinfandel Publishing.

18. Vooza. "Productivity Porn Test." *Vooza*. Retrieved from http://vooza.com/videos/productivity-porn-test/.

19. Wong, M. (2014). Stanford study finds walking improves creativity. *Stanford News*. Retrieved from 2014 http://news.stanford.edu/2014/04/24/walking-vs-sitting-042414/